It's Going to be All Right

It has become almost a cliche to refer to these times with anxious adjectives: These challenging times, these trying times, these unprecedented times, these stressful times, these times, these times, these times.

For more than a decade now, the world has gotten angrier and meaner and more afraid. Log into your favorite "social media" site, anytime, and someone will alert you about some outrage, someone will warn you about some threat, and someone will be shouting down voices of reason and calm and peace.

This book has a simple but powerful message: Never mind that the world is scary and raging; if you reach inside to a calm place, you'll find the most basic of truths: It's going to be all right. Oh, change is inevitable, and tomorrow will not look like yesterday, but it's going to be all right.

Books by Warren Bluhm

It's Going to be All Right
Echoes of Freedom Past
Full
24 flashes
Gladness is Infectious
How to Play a Blue Guitar
A Bridge at Crossroads
Myke Phoenix: The Complete Novelettes
The Imaginary Revolution
A Scream of Consciousness
Refuse to be Afraid
The Imaginary Bomb

The Roger Mifflin Collection
The Haunted Bookshop – Christopher Morley
Men in War – Andreas Latzko
Trivia – Logan Piersall Smith
The Man Who Was Thursday – G.K. Chesterton
The Demi-Gods – James Stephens
The Story of My Heart – Richard Jefferies

Also edited by Warren Bluhm
Resistance to Civil Government – Henry David Thoreau
Letters to the Citizens of the United States – Thomas Paine
A Little Volume of Secrets

For more information, visit WarrenBluhm.com

It's Going to be All Right

Reasons for hope in troubled times

Warren Bluhm

warrenbluhm.com

IT'S GOING TO BE ALL RIGHT
Reasons for hope in troubled times
© 2022 Warren Bluhm

Cover image "Blue Moon" © Marbo | Dreamstime.com
ISBN 979-8-9863331-1-3

Table of Contents

Introduction

We're living in interesting times, you and I, these past few years, aren't we? It has become almost a cliche to refer to these times with anxious adjectives: These challenging times, these trying times, these unprecedented times, these stressful times, these times, these times, these times.

I have been writing for a long time. Every full-time job I've ever held involved sitting at a keyboard and typing words into sentences, sentences into compositions. Two of my proudest possessions are the plaques declaring mine the best community columns in Wisconsin for a couple of years, way back when. Two more are the declarations that publications under my editorship were Wisconsin Newspaper of the Year for 2004 and best in its division in 2014.

I started blogging shortly after I learned there was

such a thing as a blog, around 2005. I started podcasting around the same time, because I was a radio news reporter before I was a newspaper editor and working in sound is what I did for more than two decades.

I've worked under deadline pressure so long that stress seems to be second nature to me. I found out in my mid-40s that I have high blood pressure by nature, and I take the usual medicines to keep it at non-lethal levels. Stress and me, we're old friends. Sometimes I relax and am surprised to realize how stressed I actually had been; the stress was such a part of me that it felt normal.

I say this because I know the power of this next phrase; it has stopped me in my tracks time and again:

IT'S GOING TO BE ALL RIGHT.

This world bombards us with messages to the contrary. The sky is falling, crime is rising, other countries want to destroy us, there's no time to lose, we have to do something or we're all going to die of disease, or famine, or war, or weather, or general apocalypse.

The messages are lies.

It's going to be all right.

It's going to be all right!

As I have blogged through the years, sometimes I look back and discover common themes that bubble to the surface from time to time. In the early years, faced with messages of fear and dread from politicians left and right (oh yes, these are anything but "unprecedented" times), I found myself repeating a mantra: Refuse to be Afraid. Free yourself to dream of a better life. When the merchants of fear terrorize you, rein in the impulse to be scared and remember the words of philosophers like Tom Petty, who wisely wrote, "Most things I worry about never happen anyway."

They teach you in advertising school and political seminars to scare your audience. If the audience is scared enough, they'll buy anything that promises to take away the fear. That's how snake oil gets sold by the industrial drum. That's how snakes get elected to office.

I suggested that, rather than cave to the fear, we ought to be asking ourselves: Why does this person want me afraid? What does she want from me? Is his proffered solution really going to help, or am I just surrendering my power and responsibility to a third party who will abuse them?

Those early blog posts coalesced into my first non-fiction work, a little book I called *Refuse to be Afraid. Free yourself. Dream.*

Fast forward a few years. For more than a decade now, the world has gotten angrier and meaner and more afraid. Log into your favorite "social media" site, anytime, 24/7, and someone will alert you about some outrage, someone will warn you about some threat, and someone will be shouting down voices of reason and calm and peace.

After many years of encouraging my co-workers to "do the best you can until they tell you that you can't anymore," at the end of October 2016 a somber corporate clone looked me in the eyes and told me I can't anymore. My dream job as editor of a semiweekly newspaper in Paradise was at an end. I knew it was coming; the rumors of layoffs had been in the air for a very long time. I even remember driving across the historic downtown bridge a couple blocks from the office that morning and thinking, "I wonder if this is the last time I drive over this bridge to that office." And it was. I remember a vast calm as the separation papers were handed me to sign: I had done the best I could for as long as I could until they told me to stop.

Of course, that was the end of the job, not the end of my life, and so I needed to discover the next adventure. A couple of weeks later, I went for a walk in a nature preserve not far from my former office, the aptly named Crossroads at Big Creek. I sat down at a bench not far from a crude but sturdy wooden bridge over the creek, and words came to me. I wrote:

When you are sad — for there will come a time when you are sad — remember a time you were so happy you wished the moment would last forever — because it does last forever as long as you remember it.

When you are afraid — for there will come a time when you are afraid — remember a time when you felt so safe and comfortable you knew nothing could shake your world.

When you are lost — for there will come a time when you are lost — remember a time when you reached a place that you never thought you'd reach but surprised yourself that you had it in you.

The things that shake our lives only have power when we forget the solid foundations, when we forget the solid ground we achieved before.

I realized it then, as I looked at the words that had jumped from my heart onto the page: It's going to be all right.

Those thoughts comforted me on a sunny autumn day that belied the turmoil racing through my soul, and they became a blog post and later the title piece of a book called *A Bridge at Crossroads: 101 Encouragements.*

One of my favorite artists is the singer-songwriter Sara Groves. In one of her best albums, *Add to the Beauty,* is a peaceful, quiet tune called "It's Going To Be Alright," almost a lullaby. The day I first heard the song, it struck me to the heart with its quiet reassurance, and four minutes later I was almost convinced: It's going to be all right.

We need to hear those words in our times of greatest upset, don't we? Everything's a mess, often a mess of our own making, often not, and we need someone to say it's going to be all right. We don't know how, and we fear it will get worse before it gets better, but we need to believe we will get through this, whatever "this" is. We need someone like Tom Petty to remind us most things we worry about aren't going to happen anyway. We need someone to say it's going to be all right.

And so, this book, a collection of blog posts, most of them from 2021 and 2022, a truly challenging time, in which I tried to remind you: You can do this. You will survive. Never mind that the world is scary and raging; if you reach inside to a calm place, you'll find the most basic of truths: It's going to be all right. Oh, change is inevitable, and tomorrow will not look like yesterday, but it's going to be all right.

Let me tell you what I mean.

Better time's a coming

It's going to be all right.

No one wakes up in the morning wanting to go out hate on their neighbor. No one wants the world to go to hell in a hand basket.

People want to believe the best of others — the worst of us depend on that instinct and get rich exploiting it.

People (eventually) know when they've been duped and made fools. People remember; they may not remember the details, but they know who they trust and who they don't.

At some point, when the fear mongers say, "Darkness is falling! Be afraid! Be very afraid and do as I say," a great many people will reply, "No, I don't think so."

And the sun will come up the next morning.

It's going to be all right.

It's going to be all right

It *is* going to be all right.

Everyone seems to be so agitated. Every day in the news and social media and everywhere we turn, someone is barking out another reason to be alarmed or horrified or, at least, offended. We live in ridiculous times.

But it's going to be all right.

I believe most of us live by an unconscious rule: We don't initiate force against other people. We don't intentionally hurt other people who haven't hurt us. Most people use force only in self-defense or in reaction to force that has been initiated against them. Otherwise, it's live and let live.

At some point it becomes clear that there's no reason to be so agitated — the people we're urged to hate are just folks like us who want to live and let live. And rather than stay agitated, we turn our attention back to the things that matter — caring for family, giving neighbors a hand, living and letting live.

There will still be professional agitators out there yelling, "Look at this outrage! Be offended!"

But most people will live in peace.

And it will be all right.

Darkness and light

Look, you can find darkness wherever you go. There has always been the dark. People have always been doing unspeakable things to each other for their own selfish reasons, or for someone else's selfish reasons. The challenge some days seems to be to find the light, those redeeming acts that reveal the best in people, the beauty, the evidence that something good and valued can still be found on this wretched planet.

But the plain truth is we overlook the bright and golden parts of life because they're so commonplace.

Every day, everywhere, people gather to listen to music, play or watch others play, buy groceries, exchange goods, and that's what happens: They hear music, they play, they interact. The cliche is "A plane landing safely is not news," because the simple fact is millions (billions?!) took flights or drove the roads and did not crash, went about their business and were not robbed or swindled, and made their lives better.

The seekers of darkness will show you the crashes, the thefts, the swindlers, the aberrations and abominations, but the plain and simple fact is we come in peace, we work and play in peace, and while we are constantly seeking to make it better, this life is worth living just as it is.

For every dark act, there are a thousand acts of good and mercy and light. For every killing, there are 100,000 peaceful interactions. For every act of hate, there are a million smiles and acts of love. Breaking news of horror comes from all over the world because what we encounter in our everyday lives, in the here and the now, is anything but.

Shout joy

Great poets write of wastelands and despair, of the constant-dwelling angst that haunts their souls. Not I.

I say joy — I say passion — I say love — The bursting boasting glee that dares to run where artists may plod — that cries fire and foul to the dark lords of the ego —

when I see a white-tailed deer step into the evening spotlight and catch my breath — the faltering fawn steps into the softening sunset — I laugh, and delight is the only word that springs to mind —

this green world, this green woods full of life to be savored *(life I tell you)* to embrace and to leap into the air like a child or a spry old man who remembers enough of spryness to taunt the creaky old joints and shout love into the darkening night. This is no desert devoid of humanity, this is lush this is life this is well love —

in the warmth of a hug is the secret the comfort the reality of – of – of – it all.

In the warmth of a hug is the knowledge that all is not lost, all is waiting here — right here — you feel it even if you deny — the power of the hug unleashes the tension, softens the blow of the harsh —

all is not lost — the message from eons ago waits and it is the same message from the last 5 minutes — this is life this is love — this life is about love, not the bitterness left behind by the wearing —

at the very heart of the heart of the heart — at the very deepest place in the soul of the soul's soul — in the most brilliant corner of the most brilliant mind's mind's mind — is life — is love — is passion — is hope —

I say joy, scream joy, shout joy in the life and the love and the hope. This day was grand; the next will be more so.

Once

"Today only happens once — Make it amazing."

I saw the little sign at a craft show Sunday and had to have it — especially when I saw the crafter only wanted 5 bucks for it. The message is priceless.

Today only happens once — make it amazing. Don't bog down with what could be better or what went wrong yesterday. You're only going to experience this day once, so concentrate on making it memorable (in a good way, of course).

Why stop there? This *lifetime* only happens once. Some people believe in reincarnation and new chances to get it right, but even if you do, this particular lifetime only happens once. So make it amazing. Take that chance. Reach for that star.

The ride will be worth it. And you get a new one every day — Amazing!

15

Fighting my inner zombie

"But I need to see my Likes! I should check to see if anyone reacted to my comment in Old Guys Who Like Old Comics or that thread about Madge the Palmolive Lady."

This may or may not be an exact quote, but it may as well have been, given the way I behave sometimes, scrolling and scrolling absently to see what's new in the places I lurk on social media.

My self looked at me askance. "Yesterday, when you banged your head against the dining room light fixture, are you sure you didn't hurt anything?"

"You may be right," I admitted. "I do feel a little bit like I've been dipping into the silly sauce today."

"Oh, if you feel *anything*, you're OK," my self replied. "Feeling means you're still able to shake off the social media numbness. Hey, cut that out."

"What?"

"I saw you flicking your finger up your phone screen when you're supposed to be talking to me."

"It's called swiping."

"That's a good word for it — It's always swiping your consciousness until your brain's in a coma."

"Har har. What do you suggest I do?"

"Turn that damn thing off," my self said. "The desktop, too. Write with a pen for a week. See what comes out when you're completely off the grid."

"But what if somebody calls?"

"OK, turn it on once a day, just to check your messages. Keep it off the other 23 hours and 55 minutes."

"But I need to use the electronics for work!"

My self rolled his eyes. "You can't do it, can you? You can't turn it off."

"I can't stop working!" I whined.

My self sighed. "Just stop doing social media for a week. Can you manage that?"

"A whole week?"

"Oh, for the love of Aunt Petunia. How about for an hour? and then a day? and then two, three days until you get to seven?"

"Well, maybe ..."

"Trust me, your head will clear, your eyes will defog, and your reasoning will start to get sharper."

"You're trying to suggest that scrolling endlessly through posts dulls my mind," I said.

"Duh."

"But I do learn some interesting stuff sometimes."

"You think you learn stuff by doom-scrolling."

"Well, yeah."

"Stuff like —?"

"Like I'm not the only guy who remembers Madge the Palmolive Lady."

I heard someone growl in frustration, and I'm pretty sure it was my self.

My 70th birthday

I've been spending a lot of time lately thinking about when I turn 70, even though it's little more than a year away as I write this, and sometimes I ask myself why care about it? It's going to happen anyway.

After all, I spent a lot of time over the years thinking how devastated I would be when Willow The Best Dog There Is™ dies, and it didn't make me any less devastated when my beloved golden retriever companion did, indeed, die. So why worry about being almost 70? because it will be just as surprising — no, astonishing — as I imagined it would be when it happens.

Turning 70 means I've been stumbling along for a long, long, long time — long enough to know the time left to me, be it one or five 10 or 20 or 30 years, will be a long time, too, so I'd better to get down to living it rather than wondering about how long a time has passed.

But still, what a long time has passed!

I remember "Volare" by Domenico Modugno being a new song my mom loved, and that was the summer of 1958, and I remember hearing "Calendar Girl" on my brother's transistor radio from WKBW in Buffalo, New York, and I was amazed to learn there were other radio stations in other cities far away, and that must be early 1961.

That was a long, long, long time ago, which is good to know — especially on the days when it feels like the years passed in a flash — because I have less time left to live than I have lived so far, but it all means that I have a long time left (Lord willing and the creek don't rise), which is good to know because I have a lot of stuff left to do (Lord willing and the creek don't rise).

What's that you say? The creek seems to be rising? Oh, heck. I guess I'd better get busy.

Peace for a moment

It's a busy day, spring/summer finally here, 86 degrees with a chance of thunderstorms in the near future — but for now the sun is shining.

I'm at a picnic table at a park along the water — I snap a photo to illustrate whatever blog post might come of this writing. Oh my, writing! I have so much writing to do today, after I finish here. Good thing I love to write, but even the things you love can become a chore when you have set expectations, right?

I almost have succumbed to melancholy (so much to do! so much to do!!) when a pelican soars over, flapping into the wind, standing still in the sky, apparently enjoying the interplay between his wings and the wind and the air — why else would he fight the breeze to a standstill? I imagine he is maintaining his position in the

21

air either to take pleasure in the spectacular view or to hunt the water below for his next meal. Probably the latter — pelicans need to eat, and the bay is full of lunch.

The pelican and the heat and the water and the light and the birdsong around me, and even the hum of some distant motor, all of it begins to revive me from the urge to melancholy, and instead of a procession of deadlines ahead I see the splash of a fish breaking water in the sun. I feel the wind rise and lift my light shirt away from my skin. I understand, briefly, that life is something more than an LED screen filled with words and bile and poetry and vehemence — and I feel a gentle presence (God?) and an assurance.

This picnic table may soon be drenched with rain and hail, but now — now — this moment — do you feel it, too? Now there is peace, just at the edge of this picnic table, not quite within reach but not wholly out of reach, either. The water laps the side of the seawall.

A fisherman casts his line nearby — he has different tools than the pelican but just as much hope, and hope is enough.

Wildflowers have minds of their own

Years ago, when all we had was three acres of open land and long before we built our home in 2012, I wanted to have wildflowers, so I bought an $8 box of seed that promised to cover 100 square feet with wildflowers, dug a 10 by 10 foot square in the field and scattered the box's contents.

For the rest of that summer, the square of dirt mostly remained a hapless square of dirt, with a handful of scraggly plants that did not cover 100 square feet with much of anything. It was not a success by any means.

The only memorable flower that did bloom was a fragile pink blossom with a yellow center. "Thank you," I said to that flower, "At least I got one flower out of that box."

Since then we have approached wildflowers a lot less wildly, purchasing plants after they have advanced past seed, planting them strategically and letting them go. We now have lovely areas of cup plants, compass plants, coneflowers and black-eyed Susans, among others, that have seeded and gradually grown into colorful colonies.

Funny thing, though — every so often I'll see a fragile little pink flower with a yellow center that has popped up in a random spot, a descendant of that first forlorn blossom in the 10 by 10 square of dirt, at least a decade ago now.

And this summer —

This summer, in an overgrown area so thick with woody vines and weeds that we have never bothered to try to clearing it, we have a veritable explosion of fragile pink flowers with yellow centers — dozens of them. There are also quite a few milkweed plants in that thicket, which monarch butterflies love.

It seems leaving nature alone is also a strategy.

My hapless square of dirt contributed to the overall beauty of this place after all, slowly and tenaciously and delightful-surprisingly. I gave up on that particular 10 by 10 square, which is now just another patch of grass, so the fragile little flower found another place to thrive.

Lesson learned. Beauty will find a way. Expect surprise.

Greetings, fellow people of the future

We are all living in the future — in uncharted territory. We are charting the future now.

Good morning, fellow cartographers. What will we find around this corner, over this next horizon? Isn't this exciting?

Today we will go somewhere we've never been before. This day has never happened until now. What will we find here? How will we respond?

Only one way to find out: Step forward and take a look. Remember to send a note.

Pick the right sky

"Your dreams should be as big as the sky," the weaver said.

The boy looked up from the street corner, surrounded by skyscrapers.

The girl looked up from the forest floor to see the canopy of trees, a patch of far-away blue peeking through the heavily leaved branches.

"The sky isn't very big," the boy said.

"That little sky up there?" the girl said.

The weaver finally saw the problem. He winked. And in that wink, the boy and the girl were standing in a meadow. They didn't see how it happened, they didn't feel the shift, but they saw the sky.

It was a big and blue sky, and puffy clouds dotted the expanse. They could see to the horizon, and the horizon was farther away than they had ever imagined.

"All right, then," the weaver said. "Your dreams should be as big as this sky."

He blinked again. The boy was back on the corner. The girl was in the forest among the trees.

But now they were dreaming.

The library book

What an astonishing artifact is this, with its delicate pages and the impossible date from before there was a me.

What hands have held this old tome, how many minds were touched by its story?

If there was a monster inside, how many monsters were imagined? If the monster had wings, were they scaly or feathered or rigid like a plane's? What light flashed in its eyes? If the devil had horns, were they long or short?

Even if the author supplied the details, each reader saw the monster and the other characters differently. Each moment of the story struck each reader at a different level for a different reason. It could be no other way: We each bring our own set of experiences to the table, at this unique point in our lives.

It looks like one, innocent book, lovingly or carelessly or recklessly handled by dozens or hundreds of readers, but it is as many books as hands and minds that have touched it and been touched by it.

See here

I look around my room for a book or a disc or a file to share with you: Look! See! Listen! Do you know what this object is? It is the finished product of so much work, these few hundred pages of story, this half-hour of music, this 90-minute film — someone had a story to tell, an argument to make, a desire to inspire and encourage and motivate, and here is what they created. Now dropped into a pile or stacked lovingly on a shelf, each of these objects is a time bomb waiting to be rediscovered and set off again in a willing brain with a ready heart.

Do you know how many millions of things are out there waiting to be found, and what fabulous good can be done when they are? The literal wisdom of the ages in our hands — an explosion of the greatness and vision and passion — people who overcame personal doubt and uncertainty and wrote down the thoughts and stories and dared to go forth and say, "See here! I need to share this with you. I think it's important."

And this here — this book, this music, this film — these words — this vision — this greatest story told so well —

See here. Don't look there, and don't be afraid. See what I've found, or rather see what I've rediscovered. The guy who wrote Ecclesiastes was full of despair because everything ends and comes to dust, and he concluded that means it's all meaningless, but in the transitory and the inevitable ending is where the meaning is. In a world where all things must pass, the best use of that precious time is to be kind, seek out the good, care and share the wealth of knowledge and wisdom.

Fire not the flames of hatred and anger and despair. Spark the heat of hope and compassion and understanding. Offer the open hand of friendship, not the fist, the plowshare, not the sword. Life is short enough without hastening death.

All these thousands of creations, and that's just in this one house — the books, the albums, the films, the TV shows — all of them promises against the darkness, declarations of "See here! This is important and I want to give it to you —" Souls sharing what they've learned for your delight and inspiration, and you may find this sort of collection in million of homes, likely yours, too — shouts against the darkness wherever darkness may turn.

Small stuff

Sometimes the title of the book says it all. *Don't Sweat the Small Stuff ... and it's all small stuff* by Richard Carlson is one of those.

"I'll bet that's a good book," I said the first time I saw it and the hundreds or thousands of other times I saw it since it appeared in 1997. Finally, the other day, I bought a copy at an antique mall.

Someone had inscribed it, "Katie — This is the book I was talking about. I found it very inspirational, hope you do too!! 8 Mandi 2003." Mandi drew a smile under the two dots in the exclamation points to make a smiley face.

I hope Katie got what she needed out of the book, and I thank her for passing it on, because it's as good as its title.

The book is divided into 100 little chapters of two or

three pages each, and there are brilliant little nuggets all along the way, a hundred bits of wisdom in short bursts. Here are three quotes I wrote down this morning as I went through chapters 21-25:

"If you wake up in the morning with gratitude on your mind, it's pretty difficult, in fact almost impossible, to feel anything but peace."

"We take our own goals so seriously that we forget to have fun along the way, and we forget to cut ourselves some slack."

"When you see how similar we all are, you begin to see the innocence in all of us. In other words, even though we often mess up, most of us are doing the best that we know how with the circumstances that surround us."

And there are 95 other chapters.

I can't recommend this book strongly enough.

Do what you can

So you're swamped, too much on your plate, and sure you're not going to get it all done.

Do what you can.

There will always be a to-do list longer than your ability to get it all done.

Do what you can.

You think other people on your team aren't pulling their weight? You don't know that. Maybe they're doing all they can with what's on their plate.

Do what YOU can.

Any time you spend anxious about what's not finished is time not spent doing and focusing on the task at hand.

Do what you can.

You've heard the starfish story, right? About the beach full of starfish and the guy throwing as many as he could back into the water? And a passerby says, "That doesn't matter, you can never save them all" and he holds up the one he was about to save and said "It matters to THIS one"?

Do what you can. No more, no less.

The best lives end with stuff left on the to-do list. Heck, all lives end that way.

Do what you can, while you can.

And if you can honestly say, "I did what I could," you'll be able to hold your head up.

Do what you can.

Keep doing

I had a dream where I was at a political convention, talking with an 80-something former governor who was thinking about running for governor again, and he was animated and delightfully surprised that people seemed to be excited about the idea, not dismissive.

I was hesitant to add my support because being governor is such a big job and age is a thing, but then again, if you have the energy and your mind is still there, why not keep going as long as you can?

"Do the best you can for as long as you can until you can't anymore." I used to tell nervous colleagues that when potential layoffs were hanging over our heads, except I would phrase it as "until they tell you that you can't anymore."

But in this freelance and gig economy world, this give-yourself-permission world, people have figured out that they don't have to wait until someone says they can do it, and they don't have to stop when someone tells them to stop.

Eventually the layoff people came for me and told me I couldn't do my thing anymore, but I kept doing it, just not for them — I kept doing it for me, and for you.

Keep doing your best

I told my colleagues, "Do the best you can for as long as you can until you're told you can't do it anymore." Five years after the hangman came for me, I would add, "and after they tell you, keep on doing your best."

If you still have the knack and the passion, being told you can't is not an edict; it's a challenge.

When I was laid off from my dream job reporting and editing, I took a little time to reassess, and I found myself reporting and editing again, this time because I wanted to and the community needed someone to. I continued for another four years, and I did the best I could until I couldn't, and this time it was my decision. And there's the point: It's not someone else's right to tell you to stop giving when you have more to give.

Create value. Everything you create has value, and the better your creation, the greater the value.

Of course you can

Of course you can.

Did somebody just say it couldn't be done?

Or worse, did somebody just say you couldn't do it — it's beyond your capabilities or something you shouldn't be doing, maybe when you have more experience or you're older or something?

People always have reasons why you can't do something.

But of course you can. Those other people aren't inside you. They can't know what you're capable of. They can't know how much it means for you to do this. They can't know because they literally are not you.

Of course you can. You know what it takes, or if not, you know how to find out. And you want this enough to do the research, get started and do the work.

So all those voices who say you can't do it — especially

that tiny little voice inside yourself that wonders if everyone else is right?

Ignore them.

Of course you can.

So go get started.

On hesitation

Is hesitation an instinct that protects us, or is it a demon that hates when we take action? Or is it ... Oh, it's you! Hello, fear, my old friend, are we to have this chat again? All those years of fear, and here we are on the same precipice with the same doubts and the same paralysis and the same psychoanalysis.

And all the many pauses and hemhawses and chances that passed because I didn't take them — someone said, "It's not the things you did that you'll regret, it's the things you didn't do when you could." Ain't it the truth.

But moping over lost time is yet another hesitation, another moment lost to fear and indecision. "There always will be time" is a lie. "You've got plenty of time" is a lie. Standing here talking and thinking and worrying and regretting is not doing it, either.

Don't just sit there; do something.

Get over "If only I'd done something when I had the chance," because you didn't and that's that. But now? When you have *this* chance?

Don't just sit there; do something. Do what you can, do all you can, while you can.

Fear knots

It starts when you're always afraid that if you step out of line, someone will come and take you away. And then you become afraid of being afraid of being afraid, but you don't know how to stop being afraid, and you get upset when you meet someone who doesn't seem to be afraid, because you're afraid they're not afraid.

Then someone says, "Fear not!" and you reply, "Fear knot? Damn straight! I'm tied up in fears!" but that's OK because who wouldn't be afraid at a time like this?!

These are scary times, but if you look hard enough, times are always scary. There's always some disease to catch, some moron trying to start a war, an idiot politician who thinks they can run your life better than you can, a drunk driver heading your way, an identity thief who wants to be you, an SOB who wants to steal your life savings, a dog who wants to bite your leg, and a bear in the woods.

Who wouldn't be afraid of all that? I'm getting nervous just writing about it. Never mind that most people are healthy, peaceful and willing to live and let live. Let's obsess about the psychotic, sociopathic, unhealthy rotten apples who threaten to spoil the whole barrel.

Or — maybe this is better — let's live our lives in peace and freedom, with a cautious but not panicked eye out for trouble. Let's refuse to let fear run our lives.

Isn't that a saner way to live? a healthier way to live? a better way to live? That's my humble opinion.

Making a list

"You should carry a notepad and pen around wherever you go," Red said. "In fact, I've started using the Notes feature on the iPhone."

The subject was short-term memory retention. I worry more than I should about being absent-minded. Every person of a certain age starts to do things like walk into a room and forget what they came for. But it seems to be happening with greater frequency, and more than once a day I have a Homer Simpson "DOH!" moment when I remembered something I was going to do and had to retrace my steps.

So I brought the notepad along when I went to shower and shave and such. It was great! I wrote down things like "bring the new box of kitty litter downstairs" and "come into work early on Monday" and "check the status of that upcoming trial," and I wrote down what the scale said and that we need body wash, and it was so good to write it down so I'd remember all of it.

I got dressed and came in here and fired up the computer and got ready to copy all the notes into appropriate places and take immediate action where appropriate.

Then I reached for the little notepad and realized I left it in the bathroom.

Now I'm back and ready to go down the list. Hang on a minute, I have to take the kitty litter to the basement.

Life is what happens while …

I've been sitting here for five minutes, thinking about what I could be writing, instead of actually writing.

I wonder if that's a metaphor for life: You could be living, but instead you sit and think about the life you could be living. Oh, it's important to sit and think, too, it's a form of preparing for what's ahead, but you know, I'm not writing down any of the things I was thinking about — not yet anyway. First I wanted to explore the little metaphor.

How many of us think and think about what we're going to do, until it's too late to do it? How many of us don't do anything because they think it's too late, when really there's no time like now? How many of us are so bogged down in thinking that they never understand that it's always now?

It's always time to do that thing! Why else do you think you're thinking about it?

49

Connecting without an intermediary

The old ways were about waiting to be found, waiting to be discovered, all of us diamonds in the rough looking for our big break.

The new ways are about climbing on a platform and eliminating the "middle man," going directly into the act, whether someone tells us we're ready or not, and maybe we're rougher and less polished than if some intermediary had discovered and polished us up, or maybe we're more real for the lack of polish: Maybe we're more appealing warts and all, just as long as there aren't so many warts that it's distracting.

(If I say, "Do you know what I mean?" and you don't, then there's still work to do — maybe. Maybe you don't get it but the people I want to reach will. The only sure way to find out is to keep working and keep trying to make a connection until the connection is made — you and me across the void, discovering we're not alone after all.)

Page 70

I'm writing these words on Page 55 of the current journal, having just taken a minute to number the upcoming pages through 70, even though under normal circumstances it may take a week or so before I need Page 70.

But now I wonder what I'll be thinking when I get to Page 70? I wonder what I'll write? Of course, the future person who finds this journal can just turn there now and see, and in a couple of weeks I'll be able to page back and see what it was that I wrote when I got there — but for today, it's the future.

The main reason I number the pages in advance is I've found I forget to do so, and I'll be writing along and see that I don't know what page I'm on — so lost in the scribbling that I didn't notice I was writing on an unnumbered page.

The numbers don't matter until I need to go back and find something and make a note so it's easy to find again: "Oh, that little piece about page numbers is on Page 55."

Notice I said "is" on Page 55. I almost wrote "was," but then I realized that it "is" on Page 55 and as of now it always will be, because that's where I put it.

Now I'm *really* starting to wonder what I'll be writing when I hit 70.

Etymology and hitting the fan

My dad did not use "those" words, as a rule, and so it was with some embarrassment that he told the joke.

I had purchased a 45 rpm record called "When It Hit the Fan" at a 10-cent cut-out sale (because I liked the label, I think – I was a kid). The lyrics of the song actually referred to "When *the* (something) hit the fan," but the singer didn't say what that something was, and I didn't understand the context. So Dad told me the joke.

A man takes a room on the second floor of a rowdy saloon, and during the night he had an urge for going but didn't want to walk downstairs through the crowded bar to the outhouse. He saw a hole in the floor and thought, "Ah! I'll use this handy portal."

Not long afterward he noticed it had become very quiet downstairs. Curious, he went down and the place had cleared out. "What happened?" he said, and the bartender poked his head up from behind the bar with a harried look on his face.

"Where were you," he asked, "when the $#!+ hit the fan?"

I realized this morning my dad had passed along a valuable piece of history, the origin of a common vulgar phrase, and so I pass it forward to you to preserve this important knowledge.

Beauty — and a good laugh — conquers fear

Each life is a gift from a higher power; may we accept this gift with gratitude and recognize the same miracle in others. May our gifts to others add only good and beautiful and love to their lives —

or a smile: May we greet hate and foolishness with humor and grace, because the ugly things in life wither in the face of a smile or a laugh.

It seems like TV news readers search the world for alarming things, delivering the information with voices full of alarm, and so I have been greeting their alarmist headlines on the TV with an exaggerated and alarmed, "OH MY GAWD," laughing at the fear mongers. Red may eventually be driven crazy by my constant alarmed cries, but it's my effort to remind myself that life and hope and a good sense of humor still exist and endure, sure as light follows dark and peace comes in the morning.

Resolve to add joy, beauty, humor, peace, good … Encourage the best of us, not the fearful cowering.

Meet the fear with hope, meet it with a stubborn intention to smooth the path for the next traveler along the road, a stubborn refusal to be ruffled by the potholes and cracks in the pavement.

Enough of what ails us! See what beauty surrounds us, see how much there is to love in this life that is over too soon, like a roller coaster ride returns to the starting point and we have to get out of the car and head back to the line.

Oh my gawd, what a wonderful world when we turn from fear and embrace the miracles.

Brush with greatness

I had the pleasure, moons ago, of being in the audience when the great motivational speaker Zig Ziglar spoke. He was an electrifying presence, and you walked away thinking you could accomplish whatever miracle you set your mind to accomplishing.

"You can have anything you want in this world if you just help enough other people get what they want," Zig would say. That's why I have never begrudged rich people their riches: In the vast majority of cases, that wealth represents the millions of people whose lives they made better. The cheaters and the exploiters are outnumbered by the helpers and the philanthropists.

If you had asked me, I would have said that although I watched him speak, I never met Zig Ziglar face to face. I do remember buying his book *See You at the Top* on the day I attended his talk, and I remember how he made me feel even though I was no closer to him than the balcony.

But then one day I pulled the book off the shelf to browse through it, and there, on the first page, was a handwritten inscription: "Warren / Zig Ziglar / John 15:5-7"

That nudged a vague memory of standing in line for a 10-second conversation. So yes, I met Zig Ziglar once upon a time. We shook hands. He smiled and signed my book, leaving a verse that quoted Jesus:

"I am the vine; you are the branches. If a man remains in me and I in him, he will bear much fruit; apart from me you can do nothing. If anyone does not remain in me, he is like a branch that is thrown away and withers; such branches are picked up, thrown into the fire and burned. If you remain in me and my words remain in you, ask whatever you wish, and it will be given you."

That day had a lasting impact on me, so it's odd I had to be reminded that I did get a chance to thank him for his words. Gosh, I hope I did thank him!

In a perfect world

In a perfect world I — am right here, sitting amid the clocks in the morning quiet, coaxing my hand from left to right and dropping images and cryptic symbols onto the journal page that represent the words coursing through my head.

Will future archaeologists look this page over and say, "Aha! 21st century English, we'll need to find an expert to read this," or will it make absolutely no common sense to them? "Markings in a sheaf full of thin materials, what practical use did this object have all those centuries ago?"

And where will my dust be scattered then? Up from the ashes and turned to ash.

Let's start over, shall we?

In a perfect word I am right here, sitting amid the clocks in the morning quiet, dropping images in cryptic symbols across the page. Every act of every moment of my life led me into this very chair at this very moment, when I realized this has been a pretty good life. I've always had something to eat (witness the belly), and while I've never been a superb physical specimen, I've been healthy almost all of the time for 68 years five months and two weeks.

Page turning now.

Come on now, I know I left it in here somewhere … Oh! Hi — Have you ever turned a page and completely lost your train of thought — what was I just thinking, it seemed important a moment ago, and now it's not even on my mind, just a lingering sense of whatever it is I'm feeling?

My, it's a peaceful quiet morning, though, except for the occasional screaming vehicle lifting its racing tires across the asphalt up the hill. We're down here, 40 feet from the old highway and maybe 100 feet from the new, with the biggest windows in the back, facing the trees and the water beyond. Maybe it would be perfect if there wasn't so much traffic, but the sound is background fuzz by now, these nine years after we began to settle in.

It really is a beautiful space of this big old world, a comfortable place to gather our earthly possessions to make our own. It's as perfect a world as two mortals can manage, in my humblest opinion, and by golly, I think I'm a happy guy. What do you know about that?

Ignition

Sometimes morning comes with a splash of creativity, bombs bursting in air with passion's red glare of urgent joy. Sometimes morning eases tenderly into the sun, softly whispering, "Oh gracious, is it time already?" Sometimes morning is an old dog content to sit at the top of the back stairs, waiting for her human to come out and sit next to her with his arm around her shoulders.

We all find peace in separate ways, but peace seeks us out in the morning. Something about sleep clears the mind, and in the waking hours of dawn, we know what we need and what we must do to get there, even if we can't put it into words.

This is the day it all begins. This is the day it ends. This is the day of fresh starts. This is the day of completion. This day is all you have. This day is one of thousands. This is the day the Lord has made just for you. This is the day the Lord has made for all of us. Rejoice, be glad; above all, rejoice and be glad.

This day will never come again; you will never pass this way again. Other days may come and go, but none quite like this one. The day just past is gone forever, converted to memory. The next day after this is a fragile promise, a whisper. This only is the day that shouts, "Here!"

Let the words of my mouth and the meditation of my heart be acceptable to you, o Lord, for if they are enough for the God of all creation, they are enough. Expressing that thought gives me pause, the slightest tremor of anxiety, but it seems foolish to be anxious in the shelter of God's promises.

Step forward with confidence and embrace this most wonderful day.

THIS MOST AMAZING DAY

1

This most amazing day

Moments before I drifted off to sleep the other night, as I reveled in a chance to rest after a hectic but productive day, I thought, "Thank you, Lord, for this most amazing day." For some reason I thought that would be a great thought to write about in the morning if only I could remember it. (You know the drill: "That idea was so good I'll surely remember it when I wake up." Uh huh.)

It's not original or mind-breaking, just a good positive thought: "Thank you, Lord, for this most amazing day." But I was too comfy to get up and write it down, so I repeated it a few times in my head to help me remember.

I woke up two or three times in the night, and before I rolled over and went back to sleep, I thought, "There was something I wanted to remember: Oh yeah, 'Thank you, Lord, for this most amazing day.'"

And when I sensed it must be 5 a.m. and time to get up, I thought, "Thank you, Lord, for this most amazing day. Hey! I remembered!" Not only did I remember, but I felt rested and refreshed and eager to sit down and start writing.

What a difference when you hold such a thought in your head all night, instead of the worries and cautions from here and there and up and down. What was it I wanted to remember? Oh yes: Thank you, Lord, for this most amazing day.

Focus your psyche on gratitude, love, peace, generosity, all of the things that comfort, and set aside worries and woes and nasties and anger. The bad stuff is out there and challenging, but a call to and recognition of the miracle of life clears the deck and sets the mind for positive action.

The idea (call it affirmation) sounded like naive drivel until I literally decided to try remember thinking every time I woke one night, "Thank you, Lord, for this most amazing day," and when I rose from bed the sense of gratitude was there not only in my head but in my heart and now my hands.

I really did thank God for this most amazing day: Another set of hours, another round of daylight, another burst of energy after a night's rest, another beginning, another cycle, another try, another opportunity to succeed. Thank you, Lord, for this most amazing day!

Oh, all the muss and fuss and grindly-do is all waiting to be mucked through, and I could start grumbling about it first thing, but what a difference to start the day with gratitude, to have spent each short waking in the night thinking, "I wanted to remember something, what was it? Oh, yes — Thank you, Lord, for this most amazing day."

Every end is a new beginning — Every problem is an opportunity — Every obstacle is a challenge — Even the stormiest days are most amazing. What do you gain by looking at the pile of obstacles and saying, "Oh, woe, it's a pile of obstacles"? Look up, see the horizon and know the answer is just a short journey away, a few steps down the road. What a most amazing day.

"Just another day"? "Another day, another dollar"? "Let's just call it a day"?

Do you know what a day is? A day is a microcosm: The light emerges and grows brighter and warmer, life stirs and stretches and moves, it renews itself and creates and loves and communicates, we set a purpose and a goal and follows through the best we can, and when the light begins to fade, we assess the day's triumphs and what may have fallen short, and we rest.

And for most of us another day waits on the other side of the darkness, for we are given thousands of most amazing days in a lifetime before we rest for good. How much better a lifetime if we take time to remember, so we don't forget in the morning, what an amazing gift each day is.

"I needed to remember something in the morning" — No, all day, consciously, every moment I have to reflect — Thank you, Lord, for this most amazing day.

2

This most amazing hunt

When the words flow, they flow, they race to come out, tumbling over one another. It helps to set the table with gratitude, I think, or I suspect. Call it invoking the

Muse, praying to God, whatever helps, but a dose of gratitude, a dollop of awe, a recognition of miracles, seems to go a long way toward priming the pump.

I thank God for this most amazing day!

This feels like one of those messages or themes that I was meant to deliver. This feels like one of those messages people need to receive, people need to hear, people need to consciously try to remember in dark of night when you're barely awake, "Thank you, Lord, for this most amazing day."

When I stayed in bed rather than leap up and write it down, it was a comfort to know the thought was still there, ready to be unleashed in the morning, and not just then but whenever I needed to unleash it, whenever I needed to remember.

What a most amazing day is every day! And we have thousands of them to savor — still, it is only a finite number of days when all is said and done, so best not to waste the challenges and opportunities to be tackled in the daily hunt.

The hunt is for nourishment — hunt for what will fill

your soul with happiness — "Life, liberty and the pursuit of happiness" are, after all, the first three gifts on the list of things endowed to us by our Creator. They are magic words, near-sacred words, and word represent something. Words mean something. Words stand for something.

In their best expression words are not very hard to understand. When they're parsed and overthought, the meaning disappears into obfuscation. When they just come out and say their meaning, communication and understanding happen.

Thank you, Lord, for this most amazing day! May I try to remember that thought at the beginning and end of every day, and a few times in the middle, too.

3

This most amazing existence

It is a most amazing day, thank you, Lord. I slept in longer than yesterday, but the dog did, too, and the cat did not caterwaul for her morning meal as much as usual.

The winds are calm, and the sky looks like it will allow the sunshine through — not blue but not foreboding.

Yes — "Thank you, Lord."

I don't know how it became commonplace not to believe in a higher power, as if humanity, this fragile, short-tempered species, was the smartest thing that nature could come up with. The beauty of it all, from the soft machine that is a honeybee to the crushing power of a hurricane, it all has a pattern to it that makes no sense in the absence of a designer and a meaning.

It's fashionable to suggest there is no meaning — but why build beings that each look different, like (forgive me) snowflakes, with a desire for purpose hard-wired in, if indeed it is all meaningless? "In 100 years none of this will matter" are words that comfort a soul battered by events, but it all does matter, doesn't it?

Put billions of unique individuals on a planet, each born with the power to make his or her own decisions, and see what happens. You can't predict any single one's destiny — now do the permutations to predict the planet's destiny by figuring the number of possible interactions among 7 billion souls. The math is easy: 7,000,000,000 times 6,999,999,999 times 6,999,999,998 times 6,999,999,997 and all the way down to times 2. That is the number of possible ways we can all interact at any given moment. We can say what we do doesn't matter, but like the Butterfly Effect, we can say it all matters.

Did the Lord decide this will be a calm, sunny morning over the shores of Green Bay, Wisconsin? I can't say — to me it makes more sense that he created the universe and set it in motion — but I don't have the ability to see that big a picture except in my imagination.

I do know some who want to harness some of that power would keep us all sedated if they could, our minds too muddled to see their machinations. Now I sound paranoid, but humans do study each other to figure ways to manipulate people's emotions and thoughts. Their most basic mistake is in the presumption that we are all assembly-line products who will react more or less the same to the stimuli, when those infinite permutations conspire to make us all different and fairly unpredictable.

I am not a number. I am a free man. And so are you.

Unless, of course, you are a free woman.

You always have a choice. Each moment is a choice — continue on this path or choose another? sugar in your coffee? some other substance? or none? or tea? Feed the dog or let her sleep longer? Read a book or watch a screen or mow the lawn? Thousand of choices every day.

Do you wonder why I say, "Thank you, Lord, for this most amazing day?"

4

This most amazing memory

Thank you, Lord, for this most amazing day.

This most amazing day does not begin with a trumpet fanfare proclaiming itself to the universe, unless you count a slow, steady emerging light defeating darkness as a fanfare — although you have to admit, wiping darkness off the landscape is a pretty good trick. An hour ago you couldn't see a darn thing without a flashlight of some kind, and even then shadows were everywhere, and now this most amazing day is here.

Still, by all signs this day is identical to any other day and every other day, except for the ingredients we pour into it.

Those magical supernatural ingredients — the choices we make, the people we encounter, the unexpected delights, the unexpected disappointments, the expected quotidian, the bullets dodged, the hits taken — all of them are stirred into a stew that is at once sweet and bitter, spicy and bland, epic and ordinary, and the finished chowder is assigned a date and filed into a big bin labeled "another day" or "one in a million I'll always remember."

What does it take to tip the scales for memorable? I dare say it involves starting the day with the intention to tip those scales. I am not so naive as to believe that saying, "Thank you, Lord, for this most amazing day" will make all the difference, but I am optimistic enough to believe it will make a difference.

How much difference depends on all sorts of factors. Now, all sorts of cliches are shouting for my attention as I try to make this point. Probably the predominant one is, "You can't always control what happens, but you can control your reaction."

I used to say "goddamit" a lot, and from time to time (heavens to Murgatroyd) I still do. Once upon a time, I vowed to say the less explosive "God bless America" instead. (Now, don't get all political on me, just roll with the thought that "God bless America" is a gentler oath than "goddamit.") I had to train myself out of the more vulgar habit, and I still often pause after shouting "God —" allowing a split-second to remind myself to call for a blessing rather than a damnation.

In the same way it takes some self=training to pause and remember what a most amazing day this is — one of a kind, never to be repeated exactly the same way. And isn't it a blessing that the most awful thing won't happen again? And isn't it a blessing to remember to savor the most wonderful thing that won't happen again quite like it did today?

Remember, and remember. That's what a memory is, after all.

P.S. Who is Murgatroyd anyway?

5

This most amazing dawn

Thank you, Lord, for this most amazing week. Sunday morning brings a new start, another round of seven days. Thank you, Lord, for this most amazing year. Jan. 1 brings another cycle of days and weeks and months. We are a rare set of generations, who are able to have said Thank you, Lord, for this most amazing century, a new cycle of years, and Thank you, Lord, for this most amazing millennium, a new cycle of centuries.

In truth, they are all reflections of the daily celebration — new sets of dawns, new sets of awakenings, new sets of stretching rested limbs and reaching for purpose and meaning.

A week ago I was agnostic on the concept of affirmation. Then I happened to decide I wanted to write about a most innocuous phrase — "Thank you, Lord, for this most amazing day" — and for a night I strove to remember that phrase, trying to hold onto it so I wouldn't forget it in the morning, another victim of my seeming refusal to sleep with writing implements next to the bed.

In the morning I was a prime example of the old saw, "You become what you think about," "As a man thinks, so he is." I was grateful for having held the thought all night, but more important, I was optimistically thanking God for this most amazing day. I was seeing the miracle in a new day bursting with potential. I didn't drag myself out of bed thinking, Oh, Lord, I'm stiff and sore and what am I going to write about and do I even care to write anything today. I sprang to my writing room, grabbed my journal and wrote, "Thank you, Lord, for this most amazing day."

And so I am a convert of sorts. I always bought into the concept, but now I have inadvertently discovered how to do it "right": Hold that thought. Keep in the back of your mind that there's something important you want to remember, and it will surface and sustain.

Actually, that's not quite true, is it? I have had plenty of times, mostly after vivid dreams, when I woke in the night determined to remember, only to be left with merely a vague memory of the feeling but no details when morning arrived. Why did it work this time? I can't honestly say, unless there was something divine or supernatural at play, or unless the words drilled the feeling into me, or unless the words expressed simply and efficiently a truth I'd been struggling to express for a very long time, or unless — why am I overthinking this? I'm simply glad, grateful and happy the phrase survived the night, because now I'm locked into committing that attitude to paper and to practice.

Thank you, Lord, for this most amazing day, for a new dawn, another rebirth like the thousands you gave me before and the unknown many ahead, but most of all for this one, today, when I have direct control over my actions. It's up to me to negotiate the twists and turns, and it's likely to be quite the journey, because every day is a small version of the longer and bigger journey we all travel, each in our own way. May I hold this spirit of gratitude in my heart the rest of the way.

Our mission is love

I wish you love.

I don't care who you love, as long as it's love. Love is more important than skin color, creed, gender or any other divisions.

Focus on giving love, and the rest just drops away.

They say God is love and we are made in God's image, and then they spread anything but love.

If God is love and we are made in God's image, then our best instinct is to love.

Our mission is love. Our purpose is love. So let's all get out there and love!

Give and receive

Every day we give of ourselves through our work, producing something of value that did not exist until we did so, whether it's a Quarter Pounder with Cheese or a theory of relativity. We are compensated for that work under terms that we agreed to when we signed up to perform the work.

You did not steal from me when you took my bucks in a peaceful exchange for the burger. My life was enriched because I had a decent meal, and your life was enriched because you earned a few pennies for your effort.

Please, please, please stop thinking that one of us exploited the other, or that Mr. McD exploited us both. That way lies pain and anger and resentment and hatred and all the other nasty stuff that ruins lives.

The search for one thing

My mind wanders and wanders and runs off track and down rabbit holes. So many directions and so many tracks and so many holes!

Is there an advantage to focusing on one thing? Of course there is, but there is also a time to explore and to find other options and alternatives to the one thing.

Curly, the wise old cowhand in the movie *City Slickers*, said the secret is "One thing" — but which one? How do you choose? And should you choose? Is diversification and multitasking a better choice? Jack of all trades and master of none? Or the best in the world at a certain task?

All the shiny pretty shiny-things out there to distract from what's important — or are they all as important in their own way? Dive, Forrest, dive into that rabbit hole and pay no attention to the man behind the curtain — he sends you to capture broomsticks and perhaps die, but you were brave and brought back the broomstick, didn't you? And the greater good is better for all that, isn't it?

And look over here, another shiny-thing to keep you happy until the next mission. So many rabbit holes, so little time …

My goal is to never be finished

I'm not in any hurry to move on to the next plane of existence. There's still too much I'd like to do. But I know in a perfect world, I'll leave some stuff unfinished.

"In a perfect world"? Wouldn't a perfect world be the one where everything is completed and tied up with a bow?

Nope. Don't think so.

How would it feel to say, "I'm finished. I've accomplished everything I ever wanted to do, done everything I set out to do"?

It would feel wrong, says I. There should always be something on the agenda to do next, or what's a heaven for?

We all should leave something on the table as evidence we didn't stop growing and learning and doing.

The best-case scenario is people will say, "Too bad he didn't finish this and that, but look at all this other cool stuff he did."

A mission statement worth living

While removing one pile of paper from among several one day, I found a printout of something I have posted two or three times over the years as "Gandhi's mission statement," from the writings of Mahatma Gandhi. I think I originally discovered it among sample mission statements in a Franklin Planner, back when I did Franklin Planners:

Let the first act of every morning be to make the following resolve for the day:
   • I shall not fear anyone on Earth.
   • I shall fear only God.
   • I shall not bear ill will toward anyone.
   • I shall not submit to injustice from anyone.
   • I shall conquer untruth by truth,
   • And in resisting untruth, I shall put up with all suffering.

How I hear those resolutions:

I shall not fear anyone on Earth. We are alike in so many ways, created equally with certain, unalienable rights. I have no right to infringe on another's rights, not does anyone have that right over me. Everybody poops. Everybody has hopes and dreams. Everybody deserves respect, and there is no reason to fear anyone.

I shall fear only God. I read somewhere that the original language uses the word *fear* in the way we use the word *awe* — and I am surely in awe of the wonderful creation that is this world. I would fear God's wrath if I did not believe in a God of Love, and if I were an atheist, I would fear what might happen if God were real.

I shall not bear ill will toward anyone. This is both self-explanatory and the hardest of Gandhi's resolutions to follow. The world teems with people who bear ill will toward me, if not personally, then toward their perception of people who look like me, think like me, believe what I believe, or were born where I was born. Someone I believe in once said when someone strikes you, turn the other cheek so they can also strike you there, and above all love that person. Easier said than done, but I also believe a gentle answer turns away wrath, and so I strive — and struggle — to follow this.

I shall not submit to injustice from anyone. This places me on a tightrope as I try not to bear ill will while also not submitting to injustice from those I'm most likely to bear ill will toward. It is possible, I know, to refuse to submit to injustice gently and firmly and even with love toward the person committing the injustice, even as they pile injustice upon injustice for refusal to submit, for refusal to fear them — but it is a difficult path.

I shall conquer untruth with truth. People in power are persistent liars, and confronting them with truth — for example, by pointing out the inconsistency in their lies — can throw them into a rage. But people recognize the truth when they hear it, and therefore untruth can always be conquered — eventually — by speaking truth, again, gently and firmly and consistently.

And in resisting untruth, I shall put up with all suffering. Make no mistake, following Gandhi's resolutions can lead to all sorts of persecution, pain and suffering. Mohandas Gandhi was himself murdered for being who he was, the very definition of what "all suffering" means. The funny thing is, Gandhi and his teachings have survived long after we have forgotten those against whom he struggled. That's why his "mission statement" remains so powerful almost 75 years after his death.

I would live my life with kindness

I am reading a 1996 book called *How, Then, Shall We Live?* by Wayne Muller. It was one of a dozen books I grabbed from a table in a room at an estate sale, where everything you could fit in a bag was $10. So I bought this book for pennies; it's a miraculous bargain.

Muller's subtitle is "Four Simple Questions That Reveal That Reveal the Beauty and Meaning of Our Lives." The four questions are Who am I? What do I love? How shall I live, knowing I will die? What is my gift to the family of the Earth?

I'm just past the halfway point, on the third question, and Muller has just shared an anecdote his friend Paul, who is in the final days of his life. Paul has accepted this reality but also wishes he had 10 more years so "I could really live as I always wanted."

Muller asks what Paul would do if we could give him those 10 years.

"I would be kind. I would live my life with kindness. I would be kind to children. I would teach them to be kind, too. This is all I ever really wanted to do, just to be kind, to be loving."

We all imagine how we might adjust our lives if, right this minute, we were told we would die soon, or within a matter of weeks or months, or on a specific date in, say, 2027. It focuses our attention on what's important.

Muller recalls a question in the *Bhagavad Gita*: "Of all the world's wonders, what is the most wonderful? The answer: "That no man, though he sees other dying all around him, believes that he himself will die." It's indeed a wondrous thing — and how different life would be if we felt, every day, all the time, the reality that all of us are going to die.

I have to believe this would be a kinder, gentler world. I have to believe we would be more fearless about living the lives we want to live. I have to believe most of us would try harder to live our best life, to be our best selves, and to be more patient with those around us who, after all, are just trying to live their best lives, too.

How shall I live, knowing I will die? We literally have a finite amount of time to work out the answer to that question. Best get busy.

Upon opening the gift

"Our life is not a problem to be solved; it is a gift to be opened."

I had time to sit and read Wayne Muller's chapters about Simplicity and Gratefulness shortly after I read about his friend Paul, and it seems I was in the proper frame of mind to receive the message. I feel like I could write for days, and then some, about much of it.

And almost none of it is new to me. A dear old friend, the late Lou O'Malley, once told us the secret to having a happy life is living with what you have, and here is Muller quoting Lao Tzu:

> *Be content with what you have;*
> *rejoice in the way things are.*
> *When you realize there is nothing lacking,*
> *The whole world belongs to you.*

Muller describes the desk of writer Frank Waters, a plain pine table with papers, pencils, and an old Olivetti portable typewriter, which moves me to write:

Always have a pen and paper. The electronics need to be charged, the desktop takes time to boot up. They all need to connect to Wi-Fi. The pen is always ready.

The essence of Muller's chapter about gratitude is summed up in that sentence, "Our life is not a problem to be solved; it is a gift to be opened." We spend so much time focused on what we lack — how life will be better if we can only fill that empty space — that we lose sight of the fullness everywhere else.

I have written that I work in a room surrounded by books — I once searched in vain online for the context of a Ray Bradbury quote, only to find it in a book full of essays sitting three feet above where I sat. And now, opening a book at random from a pile I nabbed at an estate sale because its title reminded me of a podcast I value, I find my heart opened to concepts I've known "headwise" for a long time.

Dorothy journeyed to Oz only to discover what she needed back at home. I keep looking for stuff only to find it was already here.

Instead of approaching life as a series of problems to solve, we need to look at our pile of gifts and start to unwrap them. Suddenly all that junk we were struggling with turns into the best present ever.

The girl in the dream

She writes songs. In fact, she had the No. 1 song in the world. The words and melody struck so many people so deeply they had to own it and play it again anytime they wanted.

She lives alone on the second floor of a two-story building. Maybe it was above a storefront, I couldn't see the details outside. All I saw was a long hallway, windows along the one side and the sun coming in. But she didn't look out the windows. She lives alone and never comes out.

The dream was about recording an album and we started talking about her, and how she could come out of the apartment anytime she wanted if she weren't so scared. I remember saying that song has made her a millionaire but she can't come out. Why is she so afraid?

What is she so afraid of?

I woke up haunted by the young woman. In the dream I was the musician making the album; we were between sessions, it seems, because the conversation was taking place outdoors, in a car. I was also the girl, because I remember that long hallway and the sunshine I couldn't bear to see and feel. The song has given her all of her material needs. All she needs now is to gather the courage and step outside. But it feels so comfortable in the apartment. She's simultaneously afraid to leave and aware there's nothing to fear. And the world loves her song.

I heard no music in the dream, but I knew: It was a beautiful song.

Melody

I went for a walk and came upon a stone chapel in the woods.

A young man was playing a guitar, and people were sitting on the floor and up in the balcony, smiling and drifting to the music.

It was a song of peace and reaching out in the darkness.

It was a song of hope and people finally getting together.

The song reached across space and time.

The song echoed against the stone walls and reverberated through the years.

And years went by, oh, how the years went by, and the chapel was abandoned and the woods reclaimed the site.

Still, the song resonates through the branches and is

absorbed in the ivies.

The echo settles behind my eyes and between my temples, until only the peace remains.

I discard the quotidian worries and hum a now-ancient tune.

When there are no words

The wind chimes are playing their random melody so loudly I hear it clearly through the window, so it must be cold and windy this morning. I haven't paid attention to them in a while, and it shows in the flaccid coolness in my heart. When I listen, when I actually hear them, the chimes soothe the savage, as does almost any tuneful vessel.

Sometimes I will sit feeling empty, sure that I'm missing something, and I'll put on some music and realize, "Yes. That was it. This is what I need."

Music says what needs to be said when there are no words. It celebrates a grand universe where melody describes order — or, in the case of the wind chimes, it describes tones of peace so deep that order is not necessary. Wind can be a harsh, vicious force or a gentle breeze, but the chimes bring beauty with every beat, every collision.

Words are blunt instruments. Set to music, the edge softens and the hope snuggles in.

The plain of unfinished dreams

He looked across the plain and saw dreams scattered everywhere — scraps of paper, aging buildings, candy wrappers, flowers planted in rows — all of them dreams, executed in varying degrees of completion.

"Pick one up."

"Which one?"

"I don't care — any of them. Pick one up."

He picked one up and examined it, turning it in his hands.

"I remember this dream! Or — no, I don't remember this dream at all. I was thinking of another one."

"What do you think of this one?"

"It's not bad. It looks promising. It's —"

"Why did you pause? What's wrong with it?"

"Well, it's not finished."

"Why don't you finish it?"

"It might not be as good as it could have been."

"Is it as good as it could be now?"

"Of course not."

"So you could only make it better if you finished your dream now."

"Hmph. You have a point."

"It's the entire point."

Object permanence

He was a simple man, or so he liked to think. He thought he was one of those guys who is born, lives for a bunch of years, and then dies without making an appreciable mark on the universe, one of those guys like the billions who had come before and the billions who would follow. Then he met his guardian angel.

"What, you wish you'd never been born?" The angel said. "I suppose I can arrange that."

And just like that, the whole universe blinked out of existence.

"Yeah, right," the simple man said. "Like I'm the center of the universe."

"Let me ask you something," said the angel. "Has there ever been something you've seen where you weren't right there in the middle of it all?"

"What you talking about?"

"Have you ever seen something except with those two eyes? Have you ever smelled something except through that nose? Did you ever grab something except with those two hands?"

"Of course not."

"So there you have it: You're the center of the universe. Nothing happens except when you're there."

"Don't be ridiculous."

And then he saw it: 7 billion universes walking about on a small planet in the Sol system. New universes bursting into existence every day, old universes fading out of existence at the same time. And every dying universe a tragedy, and every universe born a miracle.

"No, no, no, that isn't right," he said. "I'm just a simple man."

"Yes, you are," said his guardian angel, "and you are also a universe. An irreplaceable universe."

And the angel went on guarding him until the end of time.

Fix You

Enough moping. Enough complaining. Enough pointing of fingers.

The answer is within you. Don't like the way things are? Change yourself. Fix you.

You control all that you see. Work with that.

Old stuff is new again again

I just found out typewriters are cool again. There's even a documentary called *California Typewriter* about preserving and using typewriters in contemporary life.

So: Vinyl records, printed books, typewriters. Was I ahead of the curve when I purchased a couple of reel-to-reel tape recorders at the last picker sale? Are people escaping the digital, interwebbed world in favor of mechanical reproduction and analog? Clock faces, not readouts? Does it turn out after all that time makes more sense as something that constantly sweeps in a circle rather than as a set of blinking numbers?

We own (but rarely use) a 1950s-era vacuum tube radio and turntable console — it's a lovely piece of furniture — but when we moved it from one side of the living room to another the other day, we recalled on advantage of digital tech: the old stuff is very, very, very heavy in comparison.

The new stuff is definitely more convenient — all the music in the palm of your hand instead of a wall of LPs. But the LP has some heft to it; it's substantial — it's not a birdsong streaming from afar, it's a physical manifestation, with measurable weight, and a box of them will lift only with a little effort. It's harder to envision something as a physical product when it's miniaturized and nearly weightless.

Conversely, the weightlessness of music is part of its beauty. I never thought to consider a piano is a 500-pound instrument until I was on the cusp of buying one and bringing it home. It was hard to visualize, because a melody doesn't weigh an ounce.

Is it merely a sign of my advancing age that I call back to the technology of my youth? Or is there lasting value in the old methods, the ancient electronics and machines? A 1957 Chevrolet is a magnificent machine, but only if you never mind its miles per gallon, the planned obsolescence, no foldback seats, no air conditioning ... Those cars had only five figures on the odometer, because reaching 100,000 miles was improbable and 200,000 almost unheard of.

My dream car would be a Studebaker Golden Hawk on the outside, built with modern materials and technology on the inside. Now that I say that, newly minted vinyl albums seem to be crafted with more care now that they're not manufactured by the million. Perhaps there's something to be said for using the new methods to advance old tech.

Our lives are magic

I study Ray Bradbury because I wish to convey joy and wonder the way he does with his words ... or Paul Harvey.

I'll always remember Paul Harvey describing the amazing car of the future, rhapsodizing about its many features and technological wonders for three or four minutes, and then admitting he just described his new 1966 Oldsmobile Toronado.

Ray Bradbury and Paul Harvey were so good at using words to create that excitement in your chest as you breathe more rapidly because what you're seeing is so wondrous ... to call the reader or listener's attention to the miraculous right before your eyes ...

On the other side of this pane of glass, the wind howls. And the air is so cold that my flesh would freeze in minutes.

Yet here I am, barefoot, wrapped in a big comfortable easy chair, a bright light over my shoulder and springlike temperatures as I calmly write in a journal.

This is not the grateful warmth of a fire built in a cave or crude shelter. It's a cushioned bubble of comfort that my ancestors would consider luxury.

Like Bradbury and Harvey, I want to pick up the ordinary, hold it up and proclaim, "Look! See! Isn't this fine?"

So much we take for granted would have looked like magic not so long ago, and but for the hard work of mind and muscle to make it so, it would all still be possible only by magic. But the idea was conceived and the work was done, and today we reap the benefits of a better life where comfort and warmth through bitter winter is possible after all.

If we want a life even better than this, we need to conceive it and do the work. If we wish to maintain this life, we need to do the maintenance work.

While you're busy working, there's no little-to-no time to squabble over what someone else has earned ... or whether someone else has squandered ... or other petty quarrels. You just work, and the world gets better for your efforts.

Imagine a better world and get down to making it. That's all there is to it ...

But make no mistake: It's simple to say and so hard to accomplish.

But still: Do the work.

There it is

There is a word to comfort the weary. There is a balm for the hurting soul. There is a price to be paid for staying alive, and a price to be paid for dying.

To rise again when you're tired of falling, to continue the fight when you'd rather rest – is that bravery, or foolishness, or just plain acceptance and doing what needs to be done not to reach the end just yet?

It is all of those things and none. The quest for ꞓaning endures.

Love your neighbor as yourself

So someone asked Jesus, which is the greatest commandment, and he answered with two:

"This is the most important: 'Hear O Israel, the Lord our God, the Lord is One. Love the Lord your God with all your heart and with all your soul and with all your mind and with all your strength.' The second is this: 'Love your neighbor as yourself.' There is no commandment greater than these."

I think a key to that second one may be the words "as yourself." You have to have some love for yourself if you're going to love your neighbor "as yourself." And I think that explains a lot of the bad stuff in the world. People who loathe and mistreat their neighbors must be full of self-loathing, and their brutish behavior is their way of loving their neighbor the same way they (do not) love themselves.

And, you know? I had forgotten that Jesus was quoting from the Torah, the Old Testament, not just pulling those thoughts out of a hat.

"Hear O Israel, the Lord our God, the Lord is One. And you shall love the Lord your God with all your heart and with all your soul and with all your mind and with all your strength." That's Deuteronomy 6:4-5.

The second is a partial quote. The entire commandment in Leviticus 19:18 is, "Do not seek revenge or bear a grudge against anyone among your people, but love your neighbor as yourself." That kind of fleshes out the thought, doesn't it?

I'm not the most devout guy in the world, and I don't talk in these terms often, but I must say I think the world would be a better place if we adhered to those two commandments as much as possible. And from my glancing knowledge of other faiths, I think they're more universal commandments that transcend Christianity.

The act of love

It's as if a thousand voices were raised in alarm specifically to drag you in. "Why aren't you angry? You should be upset, you have to be scared if something — isn't — DONE. Many might die if it isn't changed, and by 'Many' we mean you. Be afraid, be very afraid, because they're coming for you, it's going to overtake you – Don't look back, because something may be gaining on you." (Satchel Paige?)

I call BS. I call for peace. I call for light and knowledge and peeling away the anger and the anxiety and the fear and the sadness. I call for life and letting it be.

Every One Of Us needs respect — no, actually, love is what we need. Give love and it will be given, not right away perhaps and not for a long time perhaps, but love and fearlessness — fearless love — endures. Fearless Love

Endures.

When someone strikes you, smile in love.

When someone insults you, smile in love.

They strike and they insult that which they don't understand. They wish you to join them in ignorance and anger and hate — Hatred drives violence — Violence is an act of hatred. The cycle will be broken only when we replace hatred with love, when the fist is uncurled to a hand of friendship.

Few WISH to hate. It is far easier to live in peace than to agitate emotions and fuel hatred. "Live and let live" is a simpler creed than "Yield to my will." Force is not needed to live and let live; the only energy expended is in the living. Bending a will takes agitation and even violence; relax the mind and it unfolds into peace.

When love is the impetus, others respond. The walls fall. The hatred is questioned, and the violent ones hesitate.

I say — what is it I'm trying to say? The hateful and the violent are overtaken by a sickness. The anger is a symptom of the disease. The slap and the insult are manifestations of the soul-cancer eating away at the person who slaps and insults. Try to understand.

Did I say love is easy? In its most natural state, yes — as easy as drinking in the sun and feeling the grandeur of a sunrise. In the face of hatred and violence, love can be an extreme effort — the disease is so contagious, it is easy to catch the anger and the fear and turn it back where it came from. No, love is not easy, but love is the answer.

Should we love the transgressor, love the ravager of peace and love, love the war monger and oppressor? Yes: Love. Those who love in the face of pure hatred may be ridiculed, martyred even, but the act of love will be remembered long after the purveyors of hate are dust in the wind. Love prevails. Love endures.

Above all, Love says, it's going to be all right.

www.ingramcontent.com/pod-product-compliance
Lightning Source LLC
Chambersburg PA
CBHW022101020426
42335CB00012B/777